To Peter & Silla with best wishes.

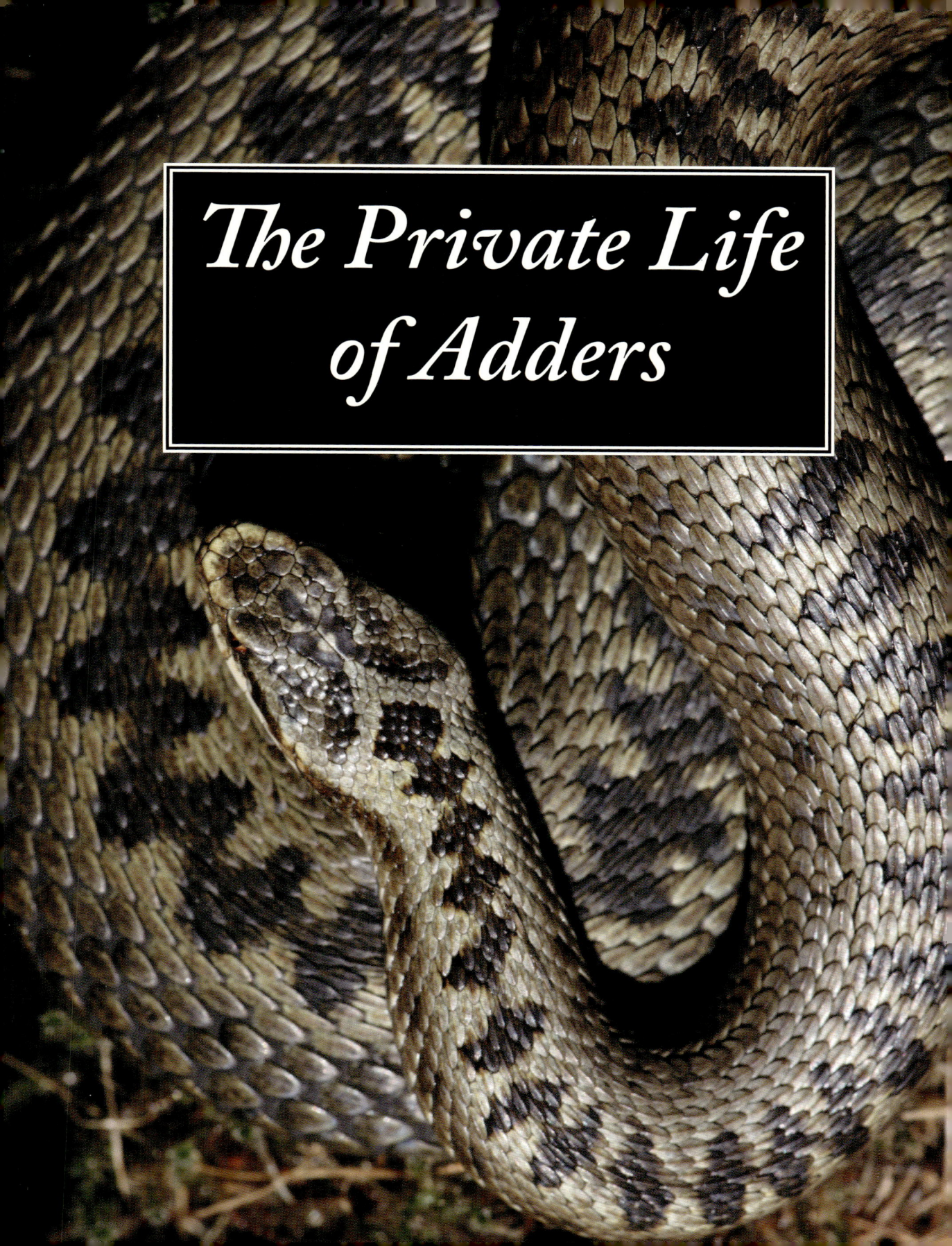

The Private Life of Adders

This book is dedicated to the memory of Peter Thurnham through whose kindness and generosity I first saw Lancashire adders

The Private Life of Adders

Rodger McPhail

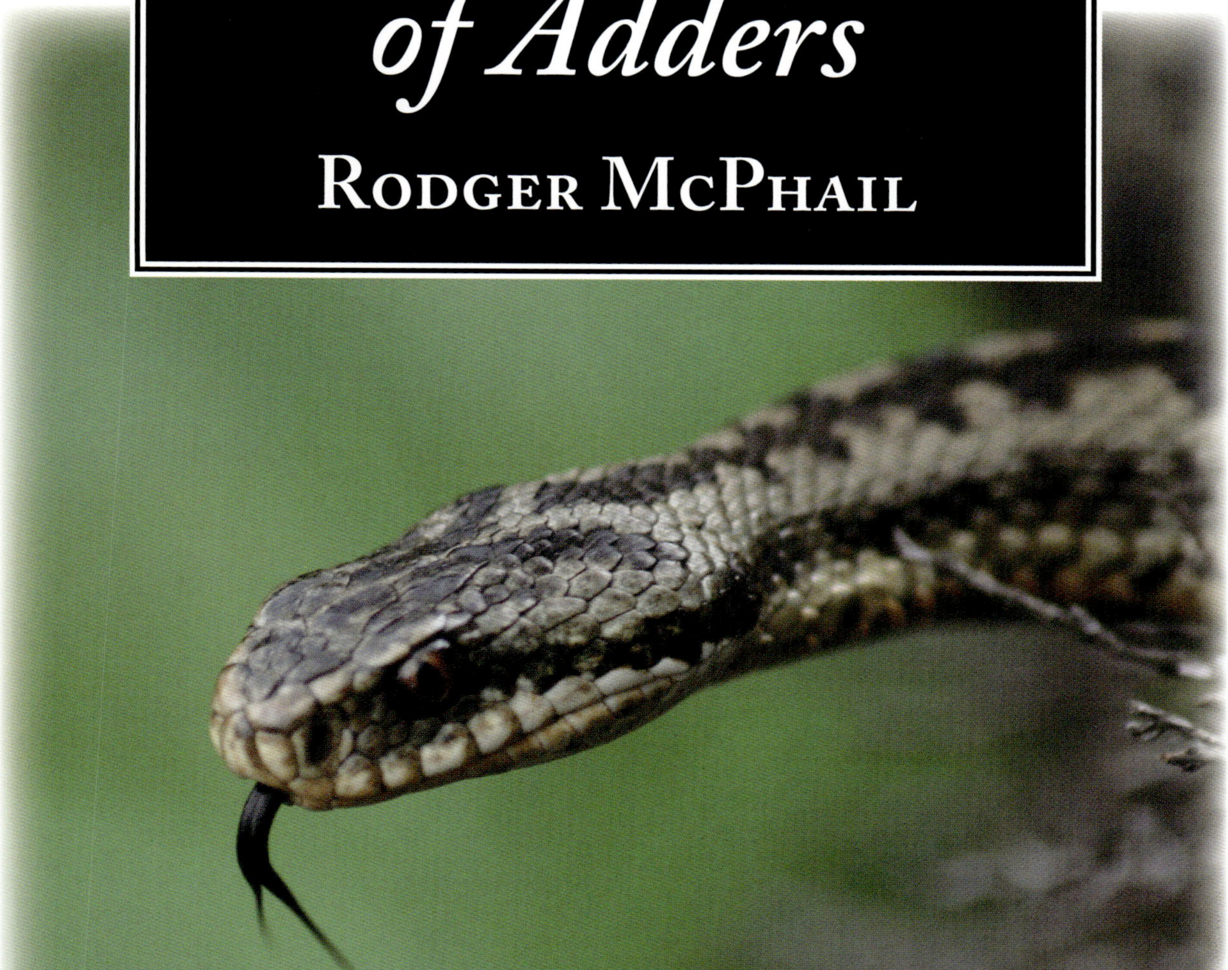

Merlin Unwin Books

First published in Great Britain by Merlin Unwin Books, 2011

Text and photographs © Rodger McPhail, 2011

Identifying Adders © Sylvia Sheldon/Chris Bradley
Habitat Management © John Baker
Moving Adders © Jon Cranfield
Are Adder Numbers Declining? © Chris Monk

All rights reserved, including the right to reproduce this book or portions thereof in any form or by any means, electronic or mechanical, including photocopying, recording, or by an information storage and retrieval system, without permission from the publisher. All enquiries should be addressed to:

Merlin Unwin Books Ltd
Palmers House
7 Corve Street
Ludlow, Shropshire SY8 1DB
U.K.
www.merlinunwin.co.uk
email: books@merlinunwin.co.uk

The author asserts his moral right to be identified as the author of this work.
A CIP catalogue record for this book is available from the British Library.

ISBN 978-1-906122-29-4

Designed and set in Palatino by Merlin Unwin
Printed and bound by Leo Paper Products

Contents

Introduction	9
Snakes in Britain	11
Locomotion and Senses	19
Basking	27
Sloughing	33
Mating	37
The Dance of the Adders	41
The Adder's Prey	47
Hunting	53
Birth & Infancy	57
A Feast of Frogs	63
Enemies of the Adder	69
Looking for Adders	75
Venom	81
Adders in Literature and Folklore	85
Neighbours	91
Further contributors *(see overleaf)*	97

Contributors

Identifying Adders by their Head Markings
    Sylvia Sheldon & Chris Bradley   97

Habitat Management for the Adder
    John Baker   101

Moving Adders to Conserve Them
    Jon Cranfield   111

Are Adder Numbers Declining?
    Chris Monk   116

Acknowledgements   125

Useful Organisations   126

Introduction

Few people are casually indifferent to snakes. There are those who find them fascinating and beautiful and those who view them with undisguised fear and loathing.

Serpents have had a bad press since Biblical times but our mistrust of them must go deeper than that. Since mankind evolved on this planet, countless numbers of us have been killed by venomous snakes. Even today, in tropical regions, thousands of people die every year from snake bites. Our fear must be a deep-rooted and instinctive one.

However, we now live in a more tolerant and conservation-minded age, and television wildlife programmes are doing their best to change our primitive attitudes to snakes, wolves, sharks and other historic villains of the animal kingdom. We are now encouraged to view these creatures with new eyes and cast off our atavistic prejudices.

The very fact that you are reading this book marks you as one of those who see in snakes a beauty, a grace and a perfection that is worthy of our admiration and respect.

I have had an obsession with snakes since I was a boy and have loved adders since I first saw one on the banks of the River Dee twenty-five years ago. More recently I discovered, to my delight, that they can be found in some numbers, in the Trough of Bowland; half an hour's drive from my home. Adders are not large animals but they have tremendous presence. They are not the sort of creature that you would give a casual glance and walk past without comment. Anyone who has been lucky enough to see one in the wild is likely to remember it for a long time.

After several years watching and photographing these splendid reptiles, I realised that I had good shots of adders doing just about everything that adders do – basking, mating, fighting, feeding etc., and it was the desire to show off my photographs that prompted me to produce this book.

Some of the text is a result of my own personal observations and the rest I have gleaned from what I believe to be reliable sources. I hope this brief monograph and the accompanying photographs will be of interest to my fellow adder enthusiasts.

Snakes in Britain

Three species of snake are found in Britain.

THE GRASS SNAKE

The Grass Snake (*Natrix natrix*), is fairly common in southern and central England, though a decline in the frog population in recent decades has had an adverse effect on its numbers. It is scarcer north of the Midlands and absent from Scotland.

There are no snakes of any species in Ireland. According to legend, St. Patrick, a herpaphobe of the most bigoted and intolerant kind, banished them in the fifth century. Perhaps St. Patrick also held a rooted antipathy for weasels, woodpeckers

Above: the grass snake

and moles – creatures also absent from the Emerald Isle.

The grass snake is a large, elegant reptile that can grow to nearly four feet in Britain and even longer on the Continent. It is drab olive, with small dark bars down the sides. The most noticeable features in the field are the pale yellow and black patches behind the head. It is semi-aquatic in its habits, living largely on frogs and toads, but it can be found in quite dry areas, such as woodland edges and meadows.

Though non-venomous, the grass snake is not without defence tactics. On being caught, its first ploy is to spray its attacker with a foul-smelling slime from its anus. Should this prove ineffective the snake will often regurgitate its last meal (a large semi-digested frog in the pocket is enough to curb the enthusiasm of the keenest schoolboy).

The last weapon in the grass snake's unpleasant arsenal is to feign death. This is does most convincingly, lying on its back with its mouth open and its tongue lolling out. Alarming though this may be to human eyes, I fail to see how this benefits the snake in the case of animal and avian predators. Surely its attacker would proceed to eat it, turning pretence into reality?

Like the adder, the grass snake hibernates through the winter months. In mid-summer it lays a dozen or so leathery eggs in rotting vegetation. The warmth generated by the decomposing plants helps with incubation.

THE SMOOTH SNAKE

The Smooth Snake (*Coronella austriaca*), though widespread in Europe, is extremely rare in England, confined to heathland in one or two southern counties. It is similar in shape to a grass snake but grey in colour and lacks the grass snake's distinctive pale patches behind the head. It lives on small mammals and lizards that it kills, python-like, by constriction.

    Not only is the smooth snake very scarce but it is secretive in its habits and rarely seen.

Above: the smooth snake

THE ADDER

The Adder (*Vipera berus*) is also known as the viper, but this name seems to be dying out in common use. The original old English name was Naedre, meaning a creeping thing. Our ancestors, on spying one, would have cried, 'Good gracious! A Naedre!' Over the centuries this evolved into 'a nadder' and subsequently 'an adder'.

The world range of *Vipera berus* is huge; from western Europe, across Russia to Mongolia and northern China. It is found further north than any other reptile.

Above: A male adder

The adder has a wide distribution throughout mainland Britain, where it inhabits moorland and heath, disused railway embankments and quarries, open woodland, chalk downs and coastal dunes. It is absent from urban areas and areas of intense agriculture. In Britain the adder is completely diurnal although in the southern extremes of its range it has been known to hunt at dusk.

A detailed description of the adder's appearance would seem superfluous in a book of photographs. Suffice to say that it is one of the very few snakes to display sexual dimorphism, the males tending to be bluish or greenish grey with black markings and the females generally duller, usually yellowish brown with dark brown markings. There is also a great deal of individual variation. The background colour can be anything from silvery white to black. Melanistic animals are not unusual. The markings on the head and neck are as individual as human fingerprints and the zig-zag dorsal marking can be anything from a thin wavy line to a series of unconnected bars.

Some males have bright orange or red on the underside of their tails. The line of dark dots along the flanks are absent in some females. The eye is red and the pupil vertical. This, with the frowning brow, gives the adder a fierce demonic expression.

In Britain a male adder can grow to about two feet and the female a few inches longer. The biggest are found in Sweden, where monsters of over three feet have been recorded. Adders can live for 30 years or more.

The Vipera are, in evolutionary terms, the most advanced of snakes. Whereas the fangs of mambas and cobras are small and stationary, the Vipera have evolved long, hinged fangs, which fold back against the roof of the mouth when not in use. Like hypodermic needles, they can inject venom deep into the body of prey.

This family includes such serpentine superstars as the Rattlesnake and the magnificent Gaboon Viper.

Rattlesnakes and pit vipers have evolved heat-sensitive organs on their faces that enable them to strike accurately at prey even in complete darkness.

A female adder

THE SLOW WORM

Another snake-like creature found in Britain, but not in fact a snake, is the Slow Worm (*Anguis fragilis*). This legless lizard is widespread and can be found in a variety of locations, including gardens, where its diet of slugs makes it a useful guest.

It is said that these benign reptiles are often mistaken for adders and killed as a result, but they are very different in appearance, being a uniformly polished bronze with no noticeable neck. On close inspection, the slow worm has a mild priest-like expression, quite unlike the devilish glare of the adder.

Above: A slow worm

The slow worm's latin name, *Anguis fragilis*, reflects the fragile nature of its tail that easily breaks off if the creature is roughly handled. Many adult slow worms have a blunt-ended appearance where the tail has been lost and partially regrown. Most lizards have the ability to shed their tails in an emergency. The newly-severed appendage thrashes about for several seconds and may save the owner's life by distracting a predator.

Slow worms, if they can avoid domestic cats and other predators, can live for over 50 years.

Below: A young male adder. Despite its fearsome reputation the adder is not an aggressive creature.

Locomotion and senses

The view that most people get of an adder is a fleeting glimpse of it disappearing into cover. Even when cold and lethargic, an adder can put on a burst in top gear if the need arises. However, no snake will use more effort than is absolutely necessary because conservation of energy is paramount importance to them.

If undisturbed and unhurried, the adder normally moves about by undulating the muscles of its abdomen and shuffling along on its belly scales. This caterpillar-like movement is often accompanied by a rather doddery shaking of the head. By this method the snake can progress in an almost straight line.

When a snake puts on a burst of speed to escape danger or chase a rival or mate, it propels itself in a series of S-shaped loops, pushing against irregularities in the terrain. This movement is beautiful to behold. The body follows the exact path taken by the head in a graceful, effortless way, giving the impression of being almost more liquid than animal. This lateral motion is also used when swimming.

Adders climb well and though not as agile as the boomslang or other tree-dwelling snakes, they can scale stone walls and bushes with ease. A snake's climbing technique is to extend the first part of the body upwards, find an anchor point and draw the rest of itself up behind. An adder can raise two thirds of its length against a vertical surface and if it can get its chin onto a branch or ledge, the rest of its body can follow. Anyone who has kept a snake as a pet will vouch that they are skilled escapologists!

The senses of serpents are very different from those of mammals. Snakes have no external ear or eardrum, so they are basically deaf. Vibrations are carried to the inner ear from

This adder is drinking raindrops off the grass. Snakes drink regularly and deeply from puddles and streams in hot weather. I have seen adders drinking raindrops off their own skin.

the ground via the jawbone, and to some extent these can warn a snake of approaching danger or prey.

At some distant stage of their evolution, snakes lived underground and lost the use of their eyes. There are examples of this type of blind subterranean reptile alive today. When serpents resumed a terrestrial lifestyle, their eyes re-developed and are different in structure from those of mammals and birds.

I have read that adders have good eyesight, but in my experience they often appear to be short-sighted and unobservant. They seem to be unable to identify objects from shape and colour and only notice prey or danger if it moves. However, they must have some close range visual sense or there would be no point in the males assuming bright breeding colours.

The most acute sense is that of smell, and like all snakes, adders smell with their tongues. The flicking tongue picks up scent particles from the air and conveys them to an aperture in the roof of the mouth, called the Jacobson's organ.

The forked tongue is a navigational aid. If one tip of the fork is collecting more scent particles than the other, it indicates the direction the snake must go. An adder will follow stricken prey by scent alone with great accuracy and persistence. The tongue is also used as an organ of touch.

An adder climbing a stone wall.

Below: A baby adder yawning. The cavity in the roof of the mouth is the Jacobson's organ. Scent particles are transferred here from the tongue.

A adder crossing a moorland stream. Adders swim well and will cross streams without hesitation if the need arises.

This is a male adder in spring, probably in search of a mate.

I have heard a first-hand account of an adder crossing the Helmsdale in Scotland at a point where the river was about thirty yards wide.

Basking

Most snakes regularly bask in in the sun and rely on its warmth to bring their bodies up to working temperature. This activity is of special importance to adders who spend a large part of their waking lives sunbathing.

Adders choose their basking spots very carefully to be at exactly the correct angle to the sun's rays, and will move several times during the day to keep in direct sunlight. Favourite basking sites are devoid of thick vegetation; a path or track or an area cropped by livestock or rabbits, but always next to thick cover into which the snake can disappear if threatened. In particularly favourable locations, several adders will often lie together in the spring, sometimes coiled on top of each other.

Adders will adopt various basking techniques according to the temperature. On cool days or in weak sunshine the snake will lie at full length or in a loose loop. To expose as much skin to the sun as possible, it will flatten its body to an almost comical degree.

As the day warms, the snake will lie in tighter coils, re-arranging itself every so often to gain the greatest benefit from the sun. On hotter days snakes will lie partially concealed by vegetation, changing position now and then to expose a different part of the body. Very hot sunshine will drive them into the shade completely.

An adder and a peacock butterfly drawn to the same sunny spot.

Male adders emerge from hibernation several weeks before the females and bask at every opportunity to build up their supply of sperm for the mating season. Pregnant females, in late summer, will bask all day, using the sun's warmth to develop their babies.

Adders are like living solar panels: they get a great deal of their energy directly from the sun. Their careful and obsessive use of its warmth has enabled them to live further north than any other snake, even into the arctic circle.

Several adders are often attracted to the same basking spot, especially if it is near to their hibernaculum.

Above: To make the most of weak sunshine, adders can flatten their bodies to a surprising degree.

Snakes have no eyelids. In bright sunshine they often shade their eyes under a coil of their bodies (see above) or in vegetation (left).

Below: This adder is shading its eye behind a single blade of grass.

When sunbathing, adders will sometimes yawn in the most impressive manner. This is not out of tiredness or boredom, but seemingly to re-align their fangs and jaws. The mouth is opened to its full extent and the fangs raised and lowered, usually one at a time, while the lower jaw is rocked from side to side. This procedure is sometimes performed after a snake has struck at prey or swallowed a meal.

In warm weather, adders will often sit out in the rain. This snake has just sloughed and the new skin is obviously very waterproof.

Sloughing

All snakes periodically shed their skins. This process known as sloughing (pronounced sluffing), occurs more frequently in young snakes that are still growing. Adult male adders will usually shed their skins shortly after emerging from hibernation; the females a couple of months later.

Before sloughing, the eyes become milky and opaque due to a secretion that separates the new skin from the old. After a few days the eyes become clear again and within a week the skin is shed.

The snake starts the process by rubbing its head sideways on the ground, loosening the skin around the lips. By pushing through vegetation, the skin is then peeled off, inside out, over the head and the front part of the body. The snake then moves along, undulating its muscles, until the skin comes off completely, often in one piece. The whole process can take as little as half an hour.

As the old skin is shed, the adder comes forth like a butterfly from a chrysalis – a splendid beast indeed! The colours are then at their brightest, the markings at their most distinct and for a day or two the skin has a soft petal-like bloom.

The papery translucent discarded skins are a good indication of the presence of snakes.

The eyes become cloudy prior to sloughing. This is due to a secretion that separates the old and the new skin.

Top left: An adder starts the sloughing process by rubbing its head sideways on the ground to loosen the skin round the lips.

Left: This snake is stretching its jaws in an effort to free the old skin.

Bottom left: Pushing into the vegetation, the snake casts the skin from its head. The transparent scales that cover the eyes can clearly be seen on the cast skin.

Below: A splendid beast indeed!

Above: A female adder sloughing. Once past the thickest part of the body, the skin comes off quite quickly, making a pleasing sound like a sweet being unwrapped.

Left: The cast skins of adult and juvenile adders.

Mating

Shortly after female adders have emerged from hibernation, those that are ready to mate that year produce a pheromone that they leave behind as a scent trail. Any male adder crossing this trail will set off in enthusiastic pursuit.

Adders can move surprisingly fast when they need to; and in short bursts, over suitable terrain, they can cover the ground at a brisk human walking pace. Receptive females tend to take up position in favoured mating spots, usually within 100 yards of the hibernaculum. It has been found that old males will make a bee-line for these chosen spots while younger snakes waste time by random searching.

Above: A courting pair of adders. During this period the male will follow the female closely wherever she goes, often resting his head on his mate as she pauses and twisting his body around hers.

Below: A splendid male adder guards his mate from rivals.

For hours the amorous male will follow the female's every move, tapping her rapidly with his chin and flicking his tongue over her body. The female responds to this by waving her tail in the air in a graceful and seductive manner.

Eventually, mating takes place and the snakes become fastened together for up to an hour. The penis of a snake is a rather alarming bulbous organ covered in hooks and spikes to ensure that it stays in place during copulation.

The male adder will stay close to his mate, guarding her against other suitors for a day or two. Should another male of similar size appear and attempt to take possession of the female during this time, a most dramatic and spectacular ritual battle will take place between the two males, known as 'the dance of the adders'.

After a couple of days 'guarding' his mate, the male adder goes off in search of another receptive female.

The hemipenis of the adder is one of a pair of male organs, only one of which is used at a time. It is equipped with hooks to hold it in place during copulation.

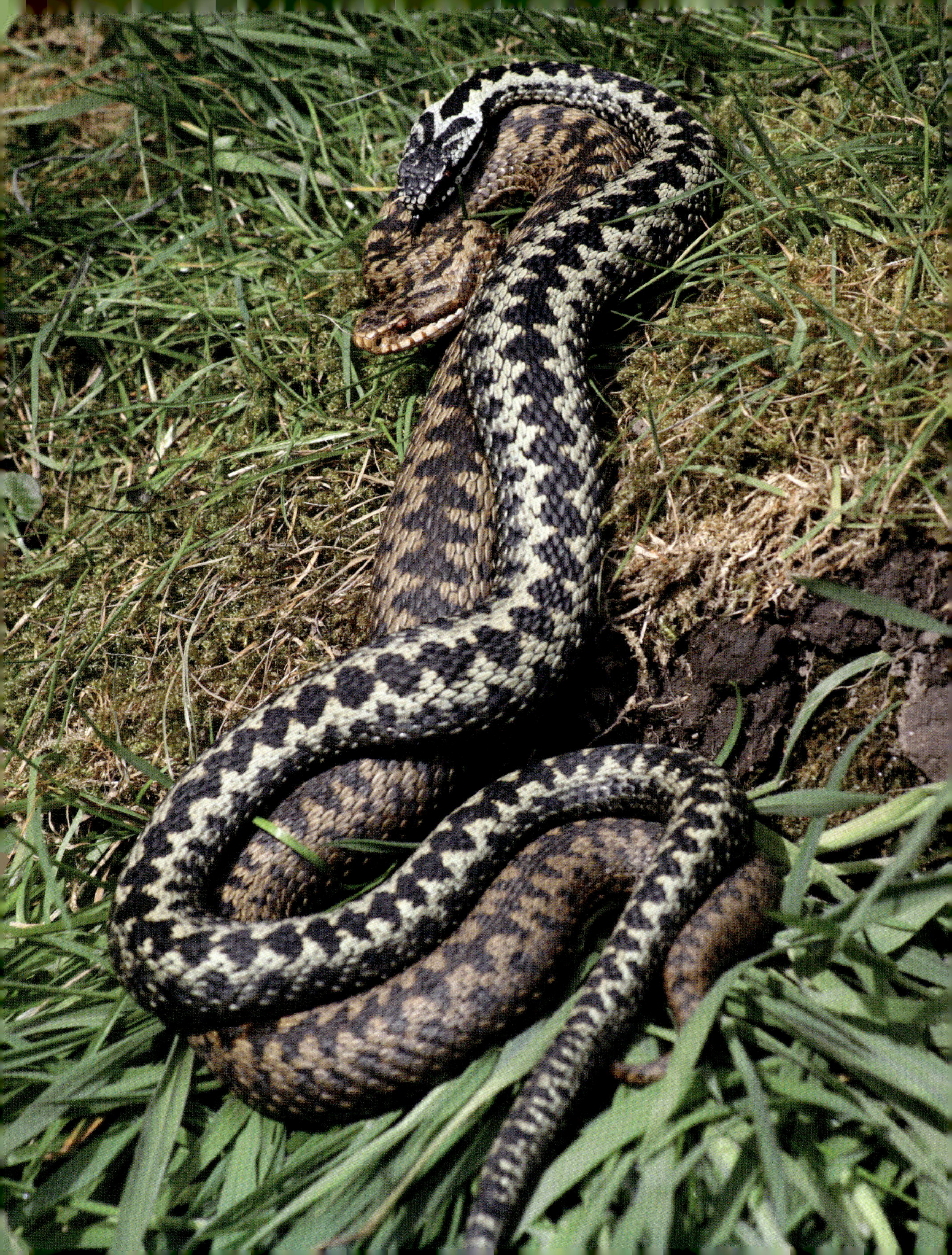

The dance of the adders

This impressive ritual is badly named, as it is quite obvious to anyone lucky enough to witness it, that it is not a dance at all, but a fight.

The two male rivals rear up side by side, swaying and weaving, each trying to get his chin on the other's head to force it to the ground. There is a great deal of rapid pushing, twisting and rolling, but no matter how heated the battle becomes, neither snake will attempt to bite the other. The opponents can become so absorbed in their combat that they are quite oblivious to human spectators, and the contest can go on for half an hour or more.

Eventually, one of the contestants will admit defeat and make off at high speed, often pursued by the victor. As snakes do not normally expend any more energy than is absolutely necessary, such frenzied jousts are most impressive.

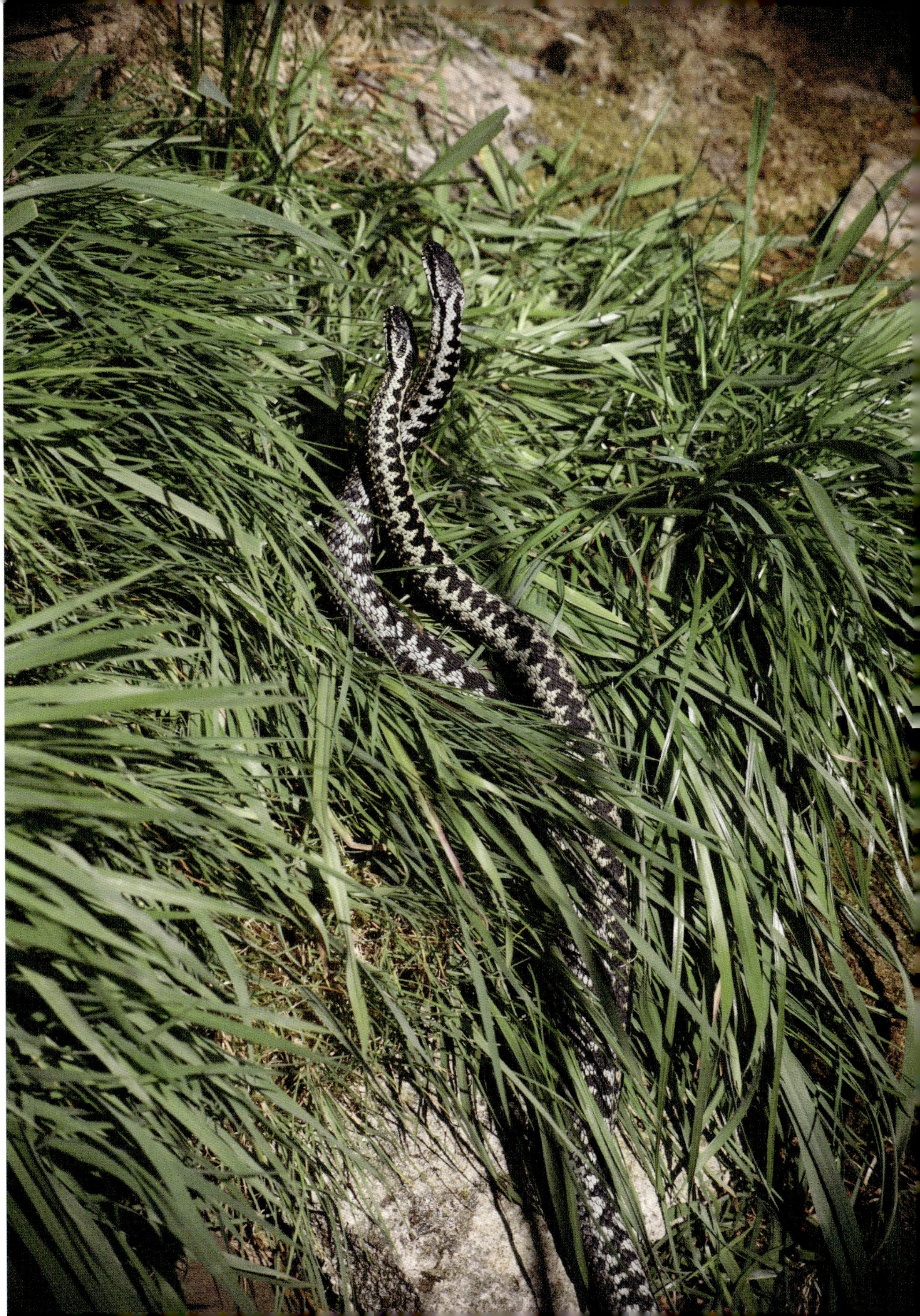

*Above: These fighting males are unequal in size.
The smaller snake puts up a very game fight against a larger intruder.*

Left: The dull colours of these rivals show that they have not yet shed their skins.

At the height of the 'dance', the twisting and writhing is almost too fast for the eye to follow.

Fighting males are vulnerable at this stage as they are oblivious to danger and their frenzied movements are likely to attract the attention of avian predators.

A third male tries to join in the combat.

The adder's prey

The prey of adders depends on what quarry species are available in that particular vicinity. If mice and voles are abundant, adders will prey on them to the exclusion of anything else. In the southern extremes of the adders' range, lizards provide a larger part of the diet. Lizards are also an important prey on acidic moorland, where small rodents are less plentiful.

I don't know if adders eat shrews; they are certainly unpoplar with predatory mammals because of their unpleasant-smelling glands. Foxes and cats will kill shrews but never eat them.

Baby frogs and newts are an important food source for little adders. Amphibians seem to be less popular with mature snakes.

It is often written that adders eat birds' eggs. I don't know if this is true or not, but as their feeding instinct seems to be triggered by movement and smell, I think it is unlikely. Adders will certainly eat the newly-hatched young of ground-nesting birds up to the size of snipe. A friend from Northumberland took a photo of a large adder struggling to swallow a golden plover chick.

Unlike predatory mammals which need a regular and constant supply of prey, reptiles are inconsistent in their eating habits. Snakes go off the feed for no apparent reason. Large pythons in captivity have been known to fast for a year or more. During these periods of abstinence, the digestive system is greatly reduced in size to save energy.

Also, unlike mammalian predators, snakes will only hunt when they are hungry. At other times, potential prey will be ignored. Mammals, in contrast, are compelled by instinct to kill, even when they don't need to – a well-fed domestic cat will still hunt mice and birds.

Surprisingly, adders will sometimes eat carrion. I once found one swallowing a slow worm that had obviously been dead for some time. It is possible that the snake had struck the slow worm and then taken several days to find it.

Common Frog
Baby frogs are an important food for young adders but the mature frog (above), while important for grass snakes, seems less popular with adders.

Toad
Toads are not a popular prey as the skin of both tadpoles and adults is toxic.

Slow Worm (top left) Adders will sometimes eat slow worms. In this instance the slow worm was lucky – the snake was not hungry.

Common Lizard (above) Adders will eat lizards. In some regions they are an important part of their diet.

Smooth Newt (left)
Newts breed in water but spend most of the year on dry land. They are preyed upon by young adders.

Long-tailed Field Mouse (left)
This mouse, along with the bank vole and the short-tailed vole, are the cannon-fodder of the countryside. All predatory birds and animals eat them. They are the staple diet of the adder.

Short-tailed Vole (left) Probably our most populous mammal, its numbers occasionally reaching plague proportions. Also known as the field vole.

Bank Vole (bottom) Like the short-tailed vole, the bank vole is a prolific breeder. The females can mate at six weeks old and can have four or five litters a year.

49

Having tracked and located a stricken mouse, the adder approaches its victim with caution to make sure it is immobilised. It then examines its prey in a leisurely manner, usually manoeuvring it into a better position, or even dragging it off, before swallowing it.

Starting at the head, the adder engulfs its victim. The skull and lower jaws are not rigidly attached but connected by elastic ligaments.

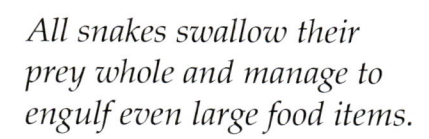

All snakes swallow their prey whole and manage to engulf even large food items.

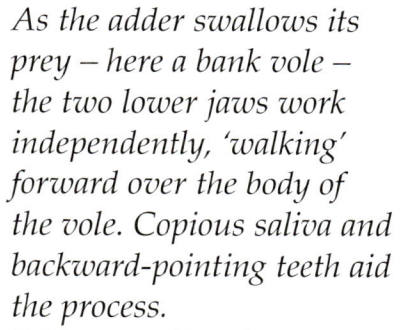

As the adder swallows its prey – here a bank vole – the two lower jaws work independently, 'walking' forward over the body of the vole. Copious saliva and backward-pointing teeth aid the process.
With a small snake and a large food item, the meal can take half an hour or more to consume.

A female adder eating a field mouse. Adders will sometimes begin to eat a mouse while it is still alive and merely paralysed by the venom.

Adders often spend some time getting their victim into the right position before swallowing it.

Mice are nearly always eaten head first.

Hunting

Adders eat very little. Six or seven months of the year are taken up with hibernation and the mating season, which leaves only a few months for hunting and feeding.

Snakes do not need to maintain a constant body heat and under normal circumstances they do not expend any more energy than absolutely necessary. This, combined with a very efficient metabolism, means that snakes can survive for a very long time without food. One large meal can last a snake for weeks. It is estimated that an adult adder only eats between five and ten voles or mice a year. Young snakes that are still growing need to eat more often.

Mice and voles make up most of the adders' diet but they will also take lizards, amphibians and young birds. In some locations adders will travel quite a distance from the hibernaculum to their hunting grounds, which tend to be low lying, damper areas.

Adders are often opportunist eaters. If a small animal wanders within striking distance of a hungry snake, it is likely to become a meal. Of the smaller mammals, bank voles, which are active during the day, are most likely to become victims this way. Field voles and woodmice are largely nocturnal and to catch these, the adder must go in search of them in their nests.

An adder strikes a mouse and immediately draws back to avoid retaliation.

Left: Moments after I took this photo, the adder was bitten by the dying mouse!
In the circumstances, the snake did not to administer another dose of venom, but patiently waited for its prey to succumb fully.

A hunting adder moves along very slowly, examining every hole and crevice, its tongue constantly flicking to catch the scent of a potential meal. On closing in on its prey the snake strikes, biting and releasing its hold in a split second. Muscular action pumps venom from glands behind the eyes, through the hollow fangs. Slow-moving or helpless targets, such as baby birds, are not envenomated at all but simply swallowed.

When a stricken rodent has dashed off, the snake usually waits a few minutes before setting off in pursuit, carefully tracking it by scent. I did once see a young adder strike a vole and take off after it like a cat!

If the victim is still alive and active when the adder catches up, it does not administer another dose of venom but patiently follows until it succumbs.

When convinced that the prey is immobilised, the adder seizes it by the nose and proceeds to swallow it. All snakes swallow their prey whole. The jaws become detached from the skull and the skin stretches to accommodate large food items. The digestive juices are very powerful and dissolve even skulls and bones of the quarry.

Once past the head, the prey is moved down the gullet by muscular action to the middle of the snake's body.

A fully-grown vole makes quite a large bulge that takes a few days to diminish.

A replete snake will bask at all opportunities, the heat of the sun helping with digestion.

Birth and infancy

Female adders are mature enough to breed at the age of three but most do not have their first litter until they reach eight years or more. The rigours of producing offspring are too great for a young snake and females that give birth in their first year of maturity do not survive the winter. Surveys have shown that an adder needs to attain a length of around 20" to survive its first brood.

After parturition, the female adder will spend the next summer or two feeding and regaining condition, before breeding again. There can be a gap of four or five years between broods. Litter size is usually 6-12, with an even ratio of males to females.

Parturition takes place in late summer. The young are

born alive, encased in a thin membrane. They are perfect pencil-sized little snakes; complete with tiny fangs and venom glands. They are very vulnerable at this stage and, as is so often the case in nature, only a small percentage survive to maturity.

As soon as they are born, the baby (neonate) adders are completely independent. The mother snake ignores her young totally and does nothing to help or protect them.

The neonates are born with internal yolk-sacs that nourish them for the first few weeks of life. When they start to feed, their favoured prey is the young of

Newborn adders. The neonates are perfect in every detail. They are similar to adults but proportionately larger in the head and thinner in the body.

*The moment of birth.
I have only witnessed parturition on two occasions.
In each case, the mother snake was slowly but constantly on the move, pausing only as each baby was born (the actual birth taking less than a minute).
The result was that the little adders were scattered over an area about two yards across, though after an hour or two they had mostly gathered in the best sunning spots.*

Above: A still-born adder.

A bluebottle, attracted to the afterbirth, indicates the size of a young adder moments after it is born.

those species that they will eat as adults; young frogs, newts, slow-worms lizards and newborn mice.

Some sources claim that baby snakes eat worms, insects and spiders. Personally, I have never seen an adder take any interest in an invertebrate.

All reptiles need to fast for several weeks before hibernation to allow their digestive systems to close down. For adder neonates born in September, this leaves very little time for hunting and many will not have their first meal until the following spring.

Baby adders show no fear of their elders and sometimes choose the same basking spots.

In both cases the neonates shed their skins very shortly after birth.

Some of the baby snakes were born free of their membranes. The first parturition that I saw produced about fourteen babies. The second was a brood of eight. In both instances, there were one or two still-births.

Left: A neonate shedding its skin less than half an hour after birth.

Below: Mother snakes show not the slightest interest in their offspring but the babies often bask near, or even on top of, adult snakes.

A feast of frogs

In boggy areas, summer brings a profusion of tiny frogs. Young adders, born the previous year, take advantage of this abundance of food and gorge on the little froglets. Baby adders seem to be more aquatic than adults. They will enter water and even totally immerse themselves in pursuit of prey. The tiny froglets are not envenomated but simply seized and swallowed. It would appear that snakes are reluctant to waste venom and reserve it for prey that is too strong for them to hang on to, or which has the potential to retaliate.

As they grow up, the young adders occasionally kill a food item that is too big for them to swallow and they are forced to abandon their meal half-way through.

A tiny adder stalks its first victim.

With good feeding, the baby adders grow quickly and at the end of their first year may be 10 inches or more in length. They start to lose their baby proportions and become miniature versions of adult snakes. Even at this early age they are very individual in markings and colouration.

A water shrew (Neomys fodiens) also joins in the feast of baby frogs. All shrews have very high metabolisms and are constantly on the move. They need to eat almost their own body weight in worms and invertebrates every day. They can starve to death if they go without food for more than four hours. The water shrew has mildly venomous saliva that enables it to tackle prey much larger than itself; up to the size of a fully-grown frog.

When the froglets become too strong and lively for the young adders to seize and swallow, the adders begin to use their venom. This frog has been bitten near its knee. The puncture mark and discolouration can be clearly seen (top photo). The frog quickly became sufficiently sluggish for the snake to proceed to eat it.

Young adders rely almost entirely on detecting movement to catch their prey.

The froglet (bottom photo) stayed motionless and the snake went past it. A moment later it made the mistake of hopping and was seized with lightning speed!

Above: The baby snakes grab their frog victims and swallow them whichever way they are facing. I believe grass snakes treat frogs the same way. Small mammals, however, are almost invariably eaten head first. The fur and legs of a mouse would make it difficult to swallow any other way.

A baby adder enters the water in pursuit of froglets. Its tiny body weighs so little that it hardly breaks the surface tension of the water.

Left: This was a fairly well-grown froglet and the snake has killed it before starting its meal.

Enemies of the adder

In spite of having a venomous bite, adders are rather vulnerable creatures, especially when they are young or newly emerged from hibernation. A wide range of predators will kill them for food.

Large birds such as gulls, ravens, buzzards and herons will kill and eat snakes and, surprisingly, so will pheasants and chickens. Pheasants are not as purely vegetarian as you might think, and infant snakes are on their menu. I once saw a hen pheasant behaving strangely and found that it had killed a large female adder, presumably out of animosity to a predator. Pheasants and chickens both originated in Asia, a continent that abounds in serpents, some of which grow large enough to be a threat to their chicks and eggs. An instinctive dislike of snakes must still be imprinted in their minds.

Above: a stoat.

Herons will kill almost anything – including adders – small enough for them to swallow whole.

The buzzard, more common in Britain than it was 20 years ago, is a predator of the adder, particularly on moorland and exposed areas where the snakes are particularly vulnerable when basking.

Hedgehogs and badgers will eat adders, and hibernating snakes must surely be at risk from weasels, stoats and rats.

It is said that deer and goats will deliberately trample adders. In Europe, wild boar are major predators of snakes. As wild boar are now found in parts of southern Britain, it may be to the detriment of adders in those areas. Adders are, of course, at risk from humans. There are still misguided individuals who will kill a snake on sight, but the main threat from Man comes from loss of habitat. Adder populations are becoming more and more fragmented due to development of land. Heavy logging machinery will impact the earth and destroy hibernating adders. Some are killed by heather

Adder arch-enemy number one – the ubiquitous pheasant. It is known to eat young adders, and to kill adult snakes out of what would appear to be sheer animosity.

burning and many die crossing roads. I saw one perish this way as it tried to cross the busy A9 in Perthshire.

Despite all these dangers, adders can still be found in good numbers in those areas that have all their requirements i.e. freedom from disturbance, a plentiful supply of prey species and suitable terrain for basking, hunting and hibernating.

A female merlin flies fast and low over grassland before seizing a snipe. These small, ground-nesting falcons live largely on pipits and skylarks. I do not think that merlins are a threat to adders. However, I have read an account of an adder trying to swallow a merlin chick.

There are stoats in the Trough of Bowland but this photograph was taken in the garden at home. This particular stoat gave birth to babies in the roof space of my studio. I can't find a reference to stoats eating adders, but I would be very surprised if they don't. They are fast and fearless and will tackle anything up to the size of a large rabbit.

The raven – an impressive corvid and one of the most intelligent birds on earth. Ravens will eat almost anything, including adders.

Adders may not have the immediate appeal of red squirrels, otters or dormice but they are charismatic and fascinating animals nonetheless and, hopefully, the growing public concern for all wildlife will be to their advantage.

The Hedgehog. These familiar animals, often seen dead on roads, frequent a wide variety of habitats, including parks and gardens. Though basically insectivorous, the hedgehog will also eat birds' eggs and chicks, carrion, amphibians and adders.
I remember, as a boy, being fascinated by a wildlife film of a hedgehog killing an adder; the snake ineffectually striking at the hedgehog's spines.

The Badger. This large, powerful creature is a mustelid – a relation of the stoat and otter. The badger takes a large variety of food, both animal and vegetable, including adders.
Badgers live communally in large underground setts, some of which have been continually occupied for centuries. Badger numbers have risen sharply in recent years. There is a great deal of controversy about their links with Bovine Tuberculosis.

Looking for adders

If you live in mainland Britain it is likely that there will be adders within a 30-mile radius of your home. Many good areas are listed on natural history websites. The best time to find them is when they first emerge in spring. Mild, still days from late March until mid-May are ideal. At this time of the year, the vegetation is still low and the snakes easier to spot.

When looking for snakes, walk slowly and carefully with the sun at your back, paying particular attention to open areas

A female adder basks in the spring sunshine. It is positioned close to shelter and protection in the form of the cleft between the two rocks.

beside thick cover. There is no need to whisper – snakes are deaf, but avoid treading heavily, especially on hard ground, as they can pick up vibrations. In early spring the snakes are often sluggish and reluctant to leave their basking places.

Should you disturb an adder and see it disappearing from view, it is worth stepping back a few yards and waiting. Often within a few minutes it will cautiously reappear and return to its basking spot.

Having seen an adder it should be possible, by moving very slowly, to get close enough for a good view. Their eyesight is not good, but sudden movement will make them take flight. To observe these perfect little creatures in the wild is a great treat. When the female adders emerge from their winter quarters, there follows a couple of weeks of activity during the mating season and you may be lucky enough to see some high speed chases and fights. At this time the male adders, consumed with lust and jealousy, are oblivious to all else and can be approached quite easily.

When you have finished admiring and photographing your quarry, it is best to retire quietly and leave it in peace. Adders should be treated with respect and disturbed as little as possible. Any temptation to try and catch one should be strongly resisted. Not only is there the danger of being bitten, but inexpert manhandling could cause them trauma or even injury.

Adders can be masters of disguise. When looking for them, it pays to walk slowly and quietly, paying particular attention to sunny spots on sheltered banks. They are seldom far from cover into which they can retreat when alarmed.

All British snakes are protected by law. It is an offence to kill or injure them or to offer them for sale. Adders do not take well to captivity and would be unlikely to survive in the sort of vivariums used to house more docile species such as corn snakes or pythons.

As summer approaches, adders become more difficult to find. The vegetation is higher and the snakes more dispersed. In some localities they seem to disappear entirely during the summer. In late August and September it is, once again, worth looking for them in the vicinity of the hiberanatum. Pregnant females are often seen basking at this time (see page 82).

This part of the Trough of Bowland in Lancashire is prime adder habitat: high, dry banks for hibernation, and lower, wetter ground for hunting.

In late afternoon this adder takes advantage of stones that have heated up during the day.

Below: A dark adder like this one stands out against its background. Completely black adders are not uncommon. The benefits a black adder will gain from absorbing heat quickly and efficiently are offset by its loss of camouflage.

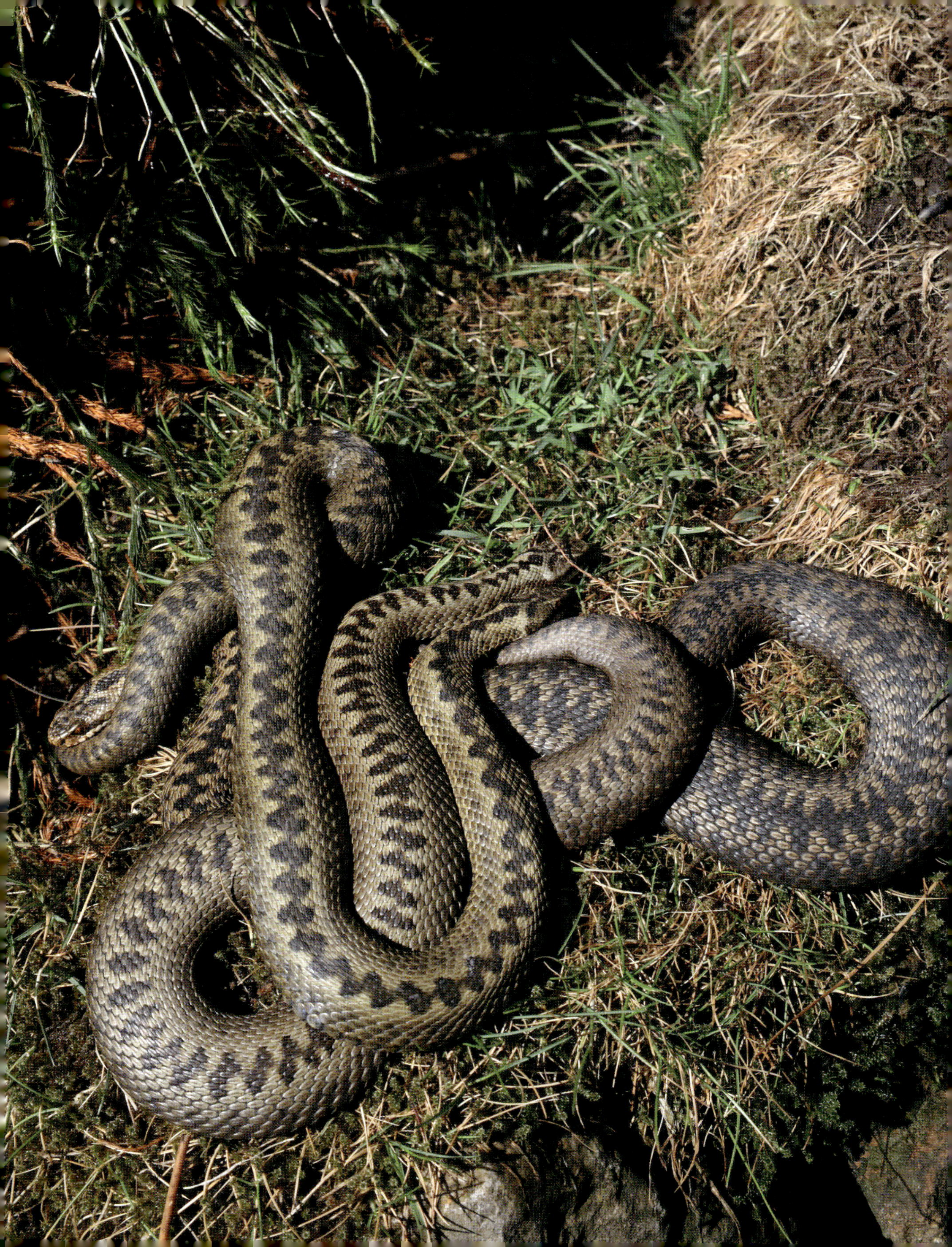

Venom

There have been several television programmes featuring enthusiastic reptile experts in shorts, intimidating, catching and handling deadly snakes. Such heroics may be very entertaining but it is inadvisable to emulate them in real life. According to statistics, 90 or so people are bitten by adders every year in Britain. In a few circumstances these are purely accidental, but in most cases it is the result of someone trying to catch a snake. The great majority of people treated for snake bites are male, which says a lot.

These incidents usually make the local press as another 'adder attack' story. This seems rather unfair to the adder which is not at all aggressive by nature and would much prefer to make good its escape.

The effects of a bite can vary a great deal. This partly depends on the size of the snake and the amount of venom used. Many defensive bites are termed 'dry', with little or no venom injected. As with insect bites and bee stings, some people have a more violent reaction than others.

Usually there is severe local pain followed, at some stage later, by swelling and discolouration. Medical help should always be sought. In extreme cases there can be grotesque swelling and blackening of the limb, spreading to the body, and a whole range of unpleasant symptoms, such as nausea, dehydration, fever, vomiting, incontinence and loss of consciousness.

Below left: An adult yawning, not a display of aggression.
Below right: Baby adders have a fully-functioning venom system.

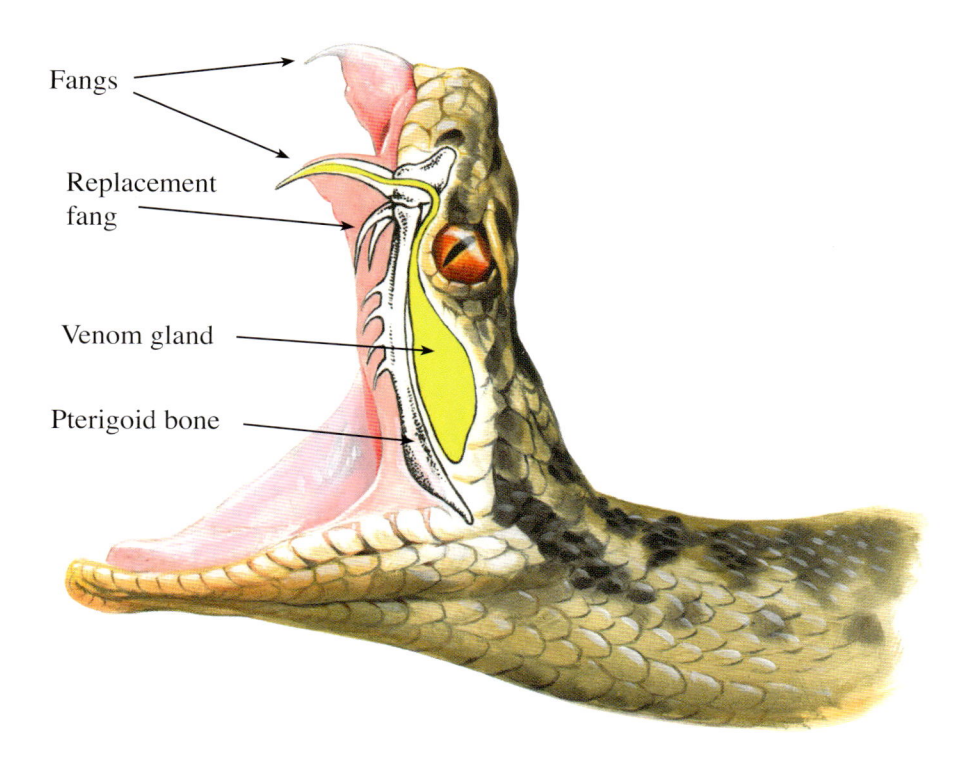

- Fangs
- Replacement fang
- Venom gland
- Pterigoid bone

When an adder strikes, the pterigoid bones of the upper jaw move forward, erecting the fangs. Venom is pumped by muscular action from the venom gland (shown in yellow) along the venom duct and down through the hollow fangs. Replacement fangs grow behind the functioning fang. Should the main fang be broken or shed, the nearest replacement fang will move forward and take its place.

However, really bad reactions are rare. To put the danger into perspective, it should be remembered that over the past thirty years, no-one has died from an adder bite in Britain. In the same time-span there have been hundreds of fatalities from bee stings and lightning strikes.

Dogs are at a particular risk from snakes as they cover much more ground and are likely to sniff at an adder if they find one. A bite can be dangerous for a dog. Veterinary help should be sought immediately.

Snake venom is modified saliva. It is made up of various proteins and enzymes and is very complex in structure. Venom from the Vipera family is mostly haemotoxin causing haemorrhaging of the blood vessels. *Vipera berus* venom is not very strong compared to other members of the group, such as rattlesnakes and puff-adders, but it is toxic enough to kill a vole in a few minutes.

An adder on the defensive. In this position, the snake can strike with astonishing speed.

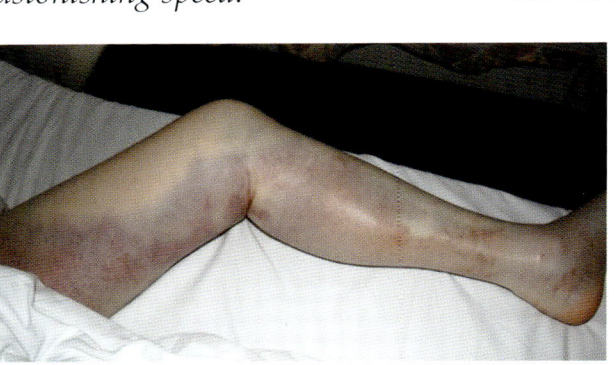

Purely to show how an adder strikes, sometimes with a sideways position of the head, this moorland specimen was provoked into striking at a balloon. It was then promptly left in peace.

Left: A typical reaction to an adder bite.

(Photo by kind permission of Consultant Plastic Surgeon Mark Moncrieff)

Adders in literature and folklore

From the Bible to Harry Potter, snakes in literature have had a rough ride. The talking serpent that led Eve astray has left a long legacy of mistrust. Almost invariably, snakes have been portrayed as the embodiment of slyness, duplicity and evil.

One of the very few examples of serpentine literary sympathy is *Snake* by D.H. Lawrence. The snake in this poem, discovered drinking at a water trough in Sicily, has regal dignity and it is the poet who is debased by the barbaric act of throwing a log at it.

Throughout the ages, many authors have specifically

referred to adders, but none as often as Shakespeare who mentions them in most of his plays. 'Adders fork' is one of the ingredients in the witches' brew in *Macbeth*, a play full of snaky symbolism.

In *Julius Caesar* we are told: 'It is the bright day that brings forth the adder, and that craves wary walking'. In *A Midsummer Night's Dream* Hermia accuses Lysander of having, 'a doubler tongue than an adder'. There is a more pleasant reptile reference in the same play, 'And there the snake throws her enamell'd skin, weed wide enough to wrap a fairy in'.

In *Hamlet* the adder is wrongfully accused of regicide, another example of undeserved bad press.

GHOST: 'Now Hamlet, hear: 'Tis given out that sleeping in my orchard, a serpent stung me. The serpent that did sting thy father's life now wears his crown'.

Shakespeare believed that a snake's flicking tongue was its sting, though he does have Hamlet talk of 'adders fang'd'. The sting fallacy dates from the Bible, 'Stingeth like an adder' (Proverbs) to W.S. Gilbert, 'Adder-like his sting lay in his tongue, his sting is present though his stung is past.' (*Princess Ida*).

Adder-like his sting lay in his tongue

'The Lord God said to the serpent, "Because you have done this, cursed are you above all wild animals; upon your belly you shall go, and dust you shall eat all the days of your life" ' – Genesis

'And there the snake throws her enamell'd skin, weed wide enough to wrap a fairy in.' – A Midsummer Night's Dream

Several authors have written of the old charcoal burners' custom of keeping an adder for good luck, notably Arthur Ransome in *Swallows and Amazons*.

Folklore is rife with weird beliefs about adders; one of the most enduring being that they swallow their young to protect them. There are written 'eye-witness' accounts of this! It was generally held that the fat of adders had medicinal properties. A wide range of ailments could be cured by it, including snake bites. Hardy refers to this in *Return of the*

Native. Brusher Mills, the famous New Forest snake-catcher, sold adder-fat ointment as a sideline.

The cast skin of an adder, worn inside a hat, was thought to cure headaches and hangovers. In Lincolnshire it was said that adders could obtain a meal by spitting venom at skylarks as they sang overhead. Before we understood the origin of

'... my schoolfriends whom I will trust as I would adder fang'd..'
– Hamlet

fossils, it was believed that ammonites were snakes turned to stone by St. Hilda.

As the adder is the only venomous reptile in Britain, our folklore abounds with such fanciful tales. These beliefs may seem ludicrous to us now, but they come from an age when people thought swallows spent the winter in mud at the bottom of ponds, pigs could see the wind, newts spat fire and wild geese hatched from barnacle shells. Our knowledge of natural history has come a long way in the last century. We no longer credit animals with weird powers and magical properties. The tendency now is to saddle them instead with human logic and emotions, which is just as misguided. Animals are fine just the way they are, without superstition and without anthropomorphism.

If we admire and appreciate wild creatures for what they are, each perfectly equipped by nature to survive in its niche and each, in its own way, beautiful, then all species, even the adder, can enrich our lives.

Neighbours

When looking for snakes in spring, an added bonus is that you are likely to see other interesting wildlife too. The adders in this book are all from the Trough of Bowland in Lancashire. They share this lovely environment with a whole range of birds, mammals, reptiles and insects.

A trip to the moors is never without incident. Even if you don't succeed in finding adders, you are bound to see something worthwhile; perhaps a dipper walking boldly into the rushing waters of the stream, or a harrier quartering the distant hillside. You may see the drumming display of the snipe or lapwings chasing crows from their nesting site. There are the evocative sounds of the moors to enjoy; the deep

Above: The bubbling springtime call of the curlew is one of the most evocative sounds in nature.

croaking of the raven, the cackling of grouse and the mad clamour of oystercatchers. On a foray in pursuit of adders, a good pair of binoculars is a boon. Not only are they useful in finding and studying the snakes themselves, but they add greatly to the enjoyment and admiration of the adders' many neighbours.

Meadow pipit (above). The commonest LBJ (little brown job) on the moors. Adders will eat the nestlings if they find them and also the young of wheatears, skylarks and other small ground-nesting birds.

Red grouse (left). The iconic king of game birds, its cackling call is the very voice of heather moorland.

Oystercatcher

A short-eared owl carrying a mouse. These ground-nesting 'bog-owls' often hunt during the day. Their breeding success depends on vole populations.

The weasel. These voracious little predators live mostly on mice and voles but they will take a variety of prey. I don't know if they will tackle snakes but I have read that large Swedish adders have been known to kill and eat weasels.

The tumbling display flight of the lapwing (above) is a glorious sight in the spring. These elegant waders thrive best on keepered moors, where foxes and crows are controlled.

The golden plover frequents estuaries and rough pastures but it nests on the moors. This bird is in its beautiful spring plumage.

These days the hare is a welcome sight but in olden times it was the subject of many dark myths and superstitions. A hare was thought to be a witch or even the devil in disguise.

The Canada geese of the Lune Valley nest up on the surrounding moors. When looking for adders in spring I have had some bad frights when these huge birds have exploded from the heather at my feet.

A favourite cage-bird in Victorian times, the linnet is now, sadly, in decline.

The stonechat (above) does not live amongst stones; it prefers gorse. The name comes from its call, which sounds like two pebbles being struck together.

Wrens (left) are found everywhere in the UK from the seashore to the mountain tops. They are one of our most numerous birds.

The skylark's exuberant cascade of silvery notes is second only to the nightingale for inspiring poets and musicians.

Along with the dipper, the grey wagtail is an archetypal bird of moorland streams.

This was a surprising sight – a carnivorous sheep! Sheep's teeth are not designed to eat meat, but this pheasant had been minced by a succession of cars and the sheep was an opportunist.

In the display flight of the snipe, the two outer tail feathers stand out at right angles and vibrate with a throbbing, bleating note.

The dainty wheatear is the earliest of our spring migrants and its arrival coincides with the first adders emerging from hibernation. Despite being as small as a sparrow, wheatears were once considered a great delicacy. They were caught in horsehair snares and sent by the thousand to fashionable restaurants.

Identifying adders by their head markings

Sylvia Sheldon and Christopher Bradley

Above: A male adder starting the sloughing process, the same distinguishing head markings showing clearly on the new skin.

A study of adders in the Wyre Forest, Worcestershire, has shown that no two adders possess identical head-markings, and that not only can they be identified by these markings but that they appear to retain these individual markings throughout their life.

The original eight-year study, undertaken by Sylvia Sheldon and Chris Bradley, which had aimed to follow the movements and seasonal behaviour of a population of adders, revealed this fact quite early on: researchers could tell individual adders apart by their head-markings alone, without the associated problems of handling and disturbance.

To investigate the possibility of adders possessing unique head-patterns, the markings on the adder head were divided into three basic components, as follows:

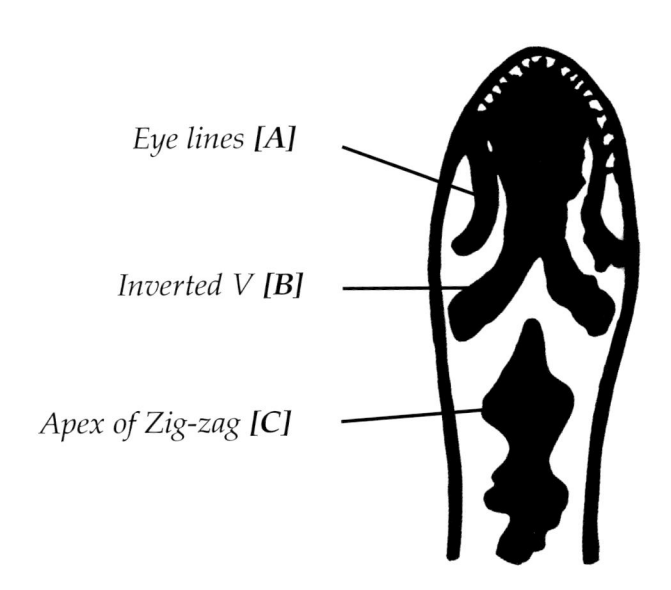

Eye lines [A]

Inverted V [B]

Apex of Zig-zag [C]

If A, B or C proved subject to individual variation, then this would provide the variables by which individual head patterns could be identified.

Colour photographs of the head of each adder were taken, all 11x13cm for immediate reference. The shed skins were also analysed, because the pigment is retained in the scale and clearly visible when viewed with transmitted light against a white background.

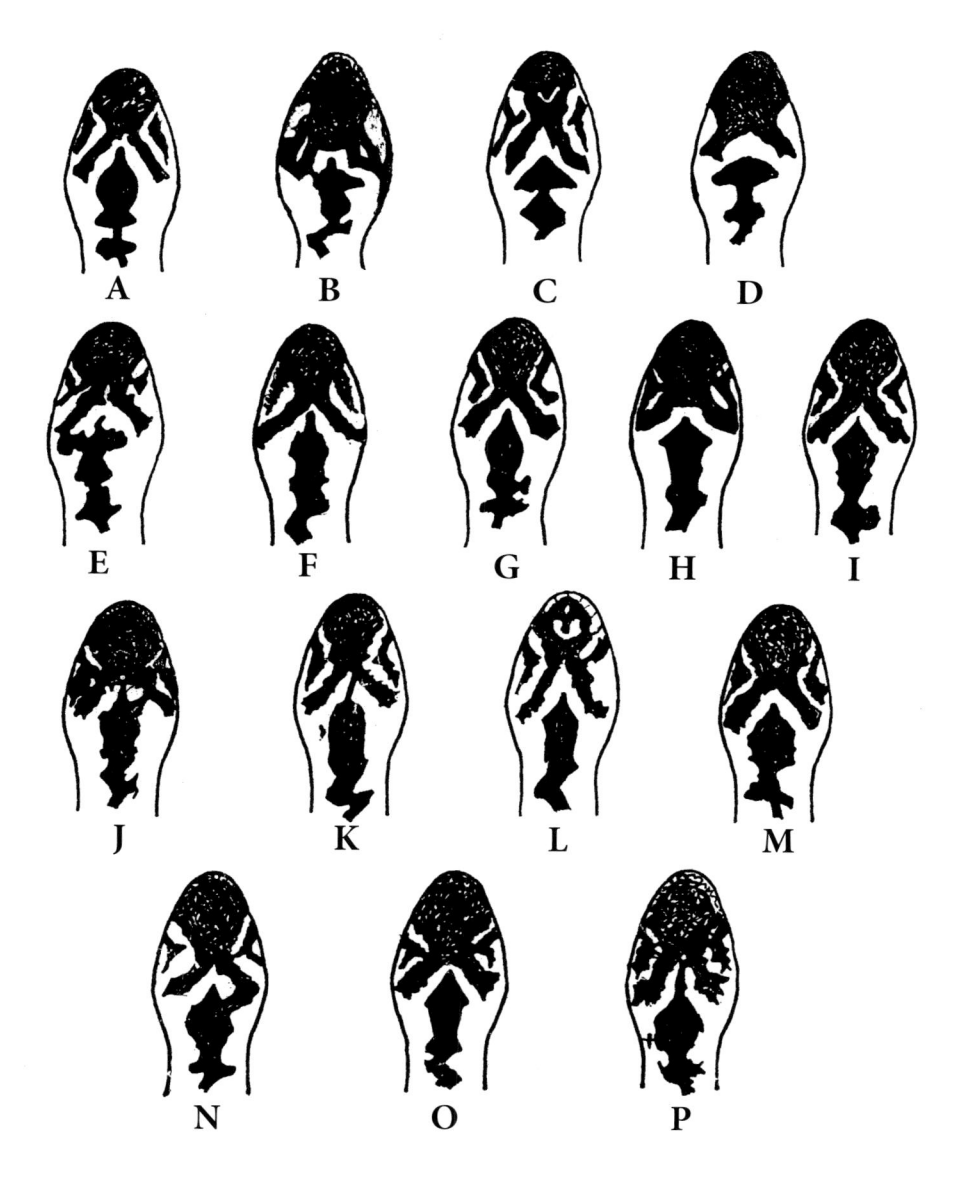

This sketch shows a selection of the 92 adders which were photographed and subsequently drawn in black and white for clearer head identification. Each one is quite distinct and varied in its head markings.

A total of 92 adders were photographed, 64 in the main study area, and the rest at various locations throughout the Wyre Forest.

Of the 92 adders, only two had identical eye-lines (A); four had identical 'inverted Vs' (B) and four had identical markings at the apex of the zig-zag (C). And only one pair out of the 92 adders had two of the three distinguishing marks the same: not one pair were identical in all three distinguishing marks.

Each of the adders in the survey was monitored over successive years for signs of alteration of their head appearance. In just one solitary male, there was a change when a single pigmented scale to the left of the apex appeared one year, when it had not been there the previous year. This was the only change detected over a period of eight years in a sizeable population of mature adders, which were regularly monitored.

Sylvia Sheldon has been studying her local populations of adders in and around the Wyre Forest, Worcestershire, for over thirty years.

Christopher Bradley has helped her with this work throughout, although his real passion is the deer population of the Wyre Forest.

Habitat management for the adder

John Baker

The adder is a creature of wild places – or at least their remnants. It has the largest range of any terrestrial snake, inhabiting from Western Europe through Asia to the Pacific coast. It is also, as reptiles go, a specialist of cooler environments, having the most northerly range of any snake, extending to just inside the Arctic Circle. In spite of this, the adder, like other reptiles, is also constrained by its thermal ecology.

As with all reptiles, the adder does not generate its own body heat, but instead relies on external heat sources. This physiology has been described as 'cold-blooded', although this term is now largely abandoned in favour of 'ectothermic'. The latter description is more accurate, because adder body temperatures are not always cold. Like most other temperate reptiles, the adder relies on heat from the sun to raise its body temperature to about 30°C. In turn this increases its metabolic rate, which is necessary to allow it to search for and digest food and to find and compete for mates.

So, in spite of its huge global range and tolerance of cooler environments, the adder requires relatively warm micro-habitats to thrive.

Adders need open habitat. That is to say, habitats where sunlight can easily penetrate to the ground, rather than shaded habitats, such as continuous woodland, where tree and understorey growth is so dense that the ground level is shaded. Open habitats allow adders to bask in the heat of the sun. Nevertheless, within a predominantly open habitat, adders still require a diverse vegetation structure, or a mosaic of patches of tall, as well as shorter, vegetation, or perhaps small patches of open ground. This is because adders also need cover. Cover is essential to allow escape from predators, as well as providing the habitat that supports the animals on which adders feed, mainly small mammals such as voles, mice and shrews. Cover also provides shelter from adverse weather conditions, such as rain, cold or extreme heat.

The combination of cover and open areas allows adders to regulate their body temperature fairly precisely. Adders do not simply lie in the sun and heat up, but they can control temperature through their behaviour. In cool conditions, early in the day, a basking adder may flatten its body by spreading its ribs, to maximise the amount of body surface exposed to the sun, rather like a solar panel.

As the snake warms, it returns its body shape to normal, exposing less surface area to the sun, hence reducing its rate of heat adsorption. As the external temperature continues to rise, there comes a point at which the snake has to move out of the sun, into shade. By altering body shape and angle to the sun, and by moving between sunny and cooler areas, an adder can maintain a fairly constant, warm body temperature. To maintain an optimum operational body temperature through behavioural thermo-regulation requires a mosaic of open areas and cover.

The warmth requirements of the adder mean that it tends to be found on free-draining soils rather than less permeable clays. Topography is also significant. Locations on south-facing slopes are warmer and sunnier than sites with a northerly aspect and so tend to be preferred. The adder is also extremely good at using topographic variation within a site, favouring sunny, south-facing slopes within a hilly or undulating location.

Habitats providing warmth and cover

The types of habitat that meet the dual demands of warmth and cover include heath, moor, scrub, grasslands and dune. Interfaces between one habitat type and another can also be exploited by adders. For example, the south-facing edge of woodland, or clearings within woodland, can provide extremely good adder habitat. Although the woodland itself may be too shaded to be of much use to adders, the trees themselves create windbreaks, and where the southern edge of woodland grades into more open scrub and, or, grassland, adders can find ideal conditions of warmth adjacent to cover.

Forestry plantations support adders in many parts of Britain. In the last century large tracts of heathland, which provided excellent conditions for adders, were converted to forestry plantation. Adders have persisted in many of these places, exploiting whatever open areas remained. Hence, adders can be found in some forestry plantations along the sunny edges of forest rides, or in clearings.

The adder's requirements can sometimes be provided by habitats recently created by humans. For example, road and rail embankments can provide sunny, well-drained sites that adders have colonised. In East Anglia, adders have taken advantage of the sea walls that have been created to protect the coast. Some of these are raised bunds (man-made embankments), which, when vegetated by rough grassland and scattered scrub, provide ideal adder habitat.

The main vegetation of much of lowland Britain is woodland. That is to say that, without the intervention of humans, much of lowland Britain would eventually become dominated by tree cover and, presumably, unsuited to warmth-loving reptiles, including the adder.

Prior to human-induced extinctions, there would also have been a range of large, wild, grazing animals present; not only deer, but also elk and wild cattle. It is difficult to determine their impact on the landscape, but it is possible that large, wild herbivores maintained sufficient open areas for reptiles to exploit. Given the historically poor state of relations between humans and snakes, it is, then, ironic that human activity has been responsible for much of the habitat that adders, and other reptiles, need. Ever since Stone Age hunters and herders burned woodland to create pasture, 6-8,000 years ago, humans have been creating and maintaining open, rather than heavily-wooded, habitats.

Habitat management

Almost all of the 'natural' habitats that we have today are created by humans. To preserve these usually requires ongoing intervention which, when carried out to benefit wildlife, is termed habitat management. Management of open, or semi-open, habitats usually takes the form of repeatedly cutting vegetation, grazing with livestock or burning. These forms of management can be, temporarily, highly disruptive to the habitat and species present. Nevertheless, without management, a great deal of adder habitat would deteriorate as it becomes overgrown by woody vegetation, and many of our most valuable wildlife sites would be degraded. To manage habitat successfully for adders, and other reptiles, requires careful application of the usual management techniques.

- Management on a piecemeal basis, by dividing a site into plots and managing only some of them at any one time will ensure that there is always some cover left for adders.
- Cutting vegetation during the winter is also likely to be less harmful than during the adders' active period, when they may be either directly harmed, or suffer from the loss of vegetation cover.
- Grazing has become a popular choice for managing open or semi-open wildlife sites. Grazing by livestock is currently used to mimic the natural grazing of wild herbivores that presumably maintained some open, or semi-open, habitats in pre-historic times. If deployed at low intensity, this management approach may be very helpful in keeping habitat in favourable condition for the adder. Unfortunately, however, conservation grazing is often too intense, using stock at densities that graze vegetation to a very short sward, so that insufficient cover remains for the adder or its prey. This situation can easily be rectified, either by lowering livestock density, or reducing the period over which a site is grazed, or dividing a site into smaller plots and grazing on a rotational cycle.

PRESERVING AND CREATING HIBERNATION SITES

One particular aspect of adder ecology that should be taken into account when planning management of sites where the species is present, is its use of hibernation sites. The adder hibernates underground. It does not dig, but instead makes use of disused rodent burrows or natural cavities, such as those created within the root systems of trees or shrubs. Sunny, south-facing banks are favoured sites. Adders sometimes hibernate communally and will return to a favourable hibernation site year after year. Hibernation sites are critically important to the adder. Not only do they allow the snakes to safely see out the winter, but that is where they may spend the majority of their time over the course of the year. On arrival of the first warm days of spring, adders, especially the males, emerge temporarily to bask. This 'lying out' period can last several weeks or even months. In some cases, mating and birth of young also take place at, or near to, hibernation sites.

A mature adder basking in overcast weather, possibly gaining some residual warmth from the stone itself.

AWARENESS OF WINTER HIBERNATION DURING BULLDOZING

Where adders hibernate communally, a great proportion of a population may be concentrated into a few locations. This can make them vulnerable to some large-scale habitat management measures that are generally scheduled for the winter. For example, if trees and scrub are to be removed to create or maintain an open habitat then, to avoid disturbance of nesting birds, this work takes place during the winter. In some cases, large areas of trees and, or, scrub are bulldozed as part of well-intentioned habitat restoration projects. Although, in general, the effects of restoring open or semi-open habitats may be beneficial to reptiles, including the adder, there is the risk that hibernating adders are bulldozed during the process. To ensure that hibernation sites are not harmed, surveys should be carried out to establish the locations of communal hibernation sites, so that these can be mapped and avoided during subsequent habitat management work.

During the type of management operations that are used to remove trees and scrub to restore or re-create heathland, not only should communal hibernation sites be avoided, but care should be taken to maintain sufficient vegetation to support adders. Specific stands of trees or patches of scrub may provide important windbreaks, creating locally warm micro-habitats. For example, adders sometimes bask on the south-facing edge of a bramble patch, or at the base of a stand of gorse or tree line. Clearing such vegetation can remove micro-habitat that is vital to adders, providing cover and warmth, especially close to hibernation sites.

THE IMPORTANCE OF BRACKEN TO ADDERS

Another target of habitat management is bracken. Bracken can be an invasive 'weed', especially on sites recently cleared of woodland.

Extensive, continuous stands of bracken outcompete other vegetation and may appear to offer little benefit to the adder, because they prevent sunlight from reaching the ground. Nevertheless, bracken can be an important habitat feature. Many hibernation sites are associated with bracken. This may, in part, be due to the fact that bracken prefers well-drained soils on unshaded sites, which are also preferred by the adder. The association may be stronger than this, though. The layer of dead 'thatch' that builds up under bracken stands may provide insulation for the hibernation site. More significantly, the dead thatch provides a warm, dry substrate on which adders bask on emergence from hibernation. So the association between adders and bracken may be significant and habitat management should take care not only to leave some bracken on site, but also to locate adder hibernation sites and ensure that these are not denuded of bracken cover.

On many sites which are protected for their conservation value, the management is often planned at the habitat level, sometimes overlooking individual species' requirements, with the exception of birds. Management at the habitat level is certainly pragmatic, because if that is got right, then the species should thrive. On some sites this may be true, but experience has shown that this is not always the case. For example, closely mowing a site on an annual basis may maintain a grassland habitat, but it may also remove reptiles, such as the adder, which cannot withstand the complete, synchronous removal of all vegetation cover.

To provide more detailed advice on the management of habitat for the adder, and other reptiles, Amphibian and Reptile Conservation has produced a *Reptile Habitat Management Handbook* (Edgar et al. 2010), which is available on request from ARC, or from the ARC website: www.arc-trust.org.

John Baker *is a Conservation Officer for Amphibian and Reptile Conservation, the wildlife organisation dedicated to native frogs, toads, newts, lizards and snakes. His work supports the voluntary network of Amphibian and Reptile Groups of the UK.*

Reference:
Edgar, P., Foster, J. and Baker, J. *Reptile Habitat Management Handbook* (2010), Amphibian and Reptile Conservation, Bournemouth.

Moving adders to conserve them

Jonathan Cranfield

One of my father's biggest regrets was that, as a teenager, he had killed adders around his home in Laindon, Essex. This was when he used to go out shooting in open countryside in what is now known as Basildon. He recalls that the adders were seen on top of molehills and grass tussocks in the fields they used to shoot. The persecution of reptiles, particularly snakes, seemed to be commonplace in the UK at this time: the opinion in many circles was that 'the only good snake was a dead snake'. Thankfully the adder, along with the other British reptiles, is now protected under the *Wildlife and Countryside Act 1981* (and its amendments in 1988 and 1991) from being deliberately killed or injured. Today my father is a passionate conservationist who has nothing to do with guns or shooting and everything to do with reptiles and their conservation in the UK. He is currently chairperson of the Essex Amphibian & Reptile Group and he spends a lot of his free time helping reptiles all over the county. He is also a key field worker for my consultancy business where he works on amphibian and reptile projects over Essex, Suffolk, Norfolk and London.

The presence of 'protected wildlife', such as reptiles, is an issue which affects land managers and developers. Reptiles can be crushed to death and harmed by heavy machinery: this is considered to be illegal if no reasonable effort is undertaken to prevent the killing and injury of these resident reptiles. Today an ecological survey is required prior to development and as part of a planning application submission to the local authority. A mitigation strategy is required when reptiles, and other protected wildlife, are affected by a development proposal. My company Herpetologic Ltd carries out ecological surveys for reptiles and devises suitable mitigation strategies for reptiles in development projects.

The most favoured approach in relation to many planning applications is to move the animals out of the way prior to the site being developed. There is clear guidance from such nature conservation bodies as Natural England as to when such measures should be adopted. The main method of dealing with reptiles in development areas is to enclose them in with plastic barrier fencing, collect all the animals up and relocate them in another suitable habitat. This poses a number of problems, the main one being: does the movement cause harm to the animals themselves? The developer is usually happy with the translocation solution, as it means he can get on with his work as soon as the reptile capture programme has been completed.

Adders in particular show a high fidelity to their hibernation or overwintering sites. I have seen adders move back to precisely the same area in which they were captured during mitigation projects. They will travel several hundred metres to do so if necessary and it seems that the plastic fence does not stop a determined female adder from getting back to her favoured basking spot for the summer. This raises particular concerns with reptile mitigation projects which involve adders. Reviews of translocations of reptiles and amphibians around the world consistently show that projects where the primary aim is conservation are more successful than translocations which are aiming to resolve a human/animal conflict. The failure of translocations is hard to determine as there is usually little follow-up work after the animals have been moved.

The success of amphibian and reptile translocations also appears to depend on the numbers of animals which are released in the first place. The larger the founding population, the more likely the translocation will be a success, according to the research. Adders are normally found in much lower numbers compared to the more frequently translocated reptile, the slow-worm, which can number many thousands in an individual project. The few hundred adders which are normally involved in a translocation may be at a disadvantage due to the low founding population.

In the UK there is very little follow-up work to determine whether these animals establish self-sustaining populations in the areas to which they have been moved. It is an issue which has concerned me over my ten-year career as a wildlife consultant. I try to move snakes only as a last resort within my mitigation work for development.

As an external advisor to a reptile mitigation project on the Norfolk Broads, I have had an opportunity to influence the decision-making process in relation to mitigation involving adders. The reptiles overwinter on flood defence banks within the heart of the Broads. The Broadlands Environmental Project has been looking at the issue of reptiles since 2004, and adders in particular have been surveyed over 2008 and 2009.

An extensive survey revealed populations of adders in locations around rough vegetation such as bramble, reed beds and woodland edges along the crest of the embankments. Mitigation works have been stipulated for these adder populations. Following best practice, the redevelopment works were modified to avoid the most important areas for these animals. They reversed their plans to strip large areas of grassland with heavy machinery, and instead used sheet piles on the front of the embankment to avoid any impact on individual animals.

Not all the adders were completely safe though and it was decided that the animals which were in most danger would be moved to safety over short distances prior to works in the autumn.

Adders have a distinct lifecycle and it was felt appropriate to try and move the animals when they were docile in the spring months. Adders are concentrated in small areas during the spring after emergence from hibernation so it was hoped that the majority of them would have been moved to safety prior to the works starting.

A series of 'replacement' habitats were constructed in the autumn 2009. The habitats took on the structure of the flood embankments and incorporated an area of water and a small area of marshy grassland. The new banks were made from local materials, utilising straw bales, Norfolk reed bundles, brash, logs and soil. The soil was provided by creating a wetland habitat alongside the hibernation bank or habitat. The resultant habitat is a microcosm of the habitat where the adders were found during the previous two years' surveys: a piece of high free draining ground for hibernation, a marshy area and a water feature which mimicked the soke dyke found along the flood defence banks.

The adders were captured by hand, as they were lying out in the early spring sun, placed into cloth bags and carried to the new habitats roughly 800 metres away from the main work areas and into the new habitats which had been constructed the autumn before.

As mentioned, the problem with moving adult snakes is their tendency to move back to the place they were originally captured – a problem when short distances are involved and possibly more so for snakes which have been moved over much larger distances.

Evidence from translocations of other reptile species suggested that 'penning in' relocated animals for a period of time enables the animals to develop a stronger fidelity to their new home.

The new habitat banks, ditches and marshy grassland were therefore enclosed within a reptile fence dug into the ground. Each adder within the enclosure was measured, weighed, photographed and marked with a non-toxic paint. In the first release pen, the adders were marked with red dots; while the second release pen had adders with yellow paint marks.

The adders were regularly monitored each time new arrivals were released into the pens. The idea was to enable the animals to settle and go through their natural spring behaviour. Once the males had finished mating, the fencing was removed to allow the males to disperse into the surrounding landscape. Over 100 adders were moved in this way and it was found that the majority of the animals settled on the new banks although some snakes were more nomadic, particularly the males prior to the females being placed into the pens. Once a few females were in the same pen, the males seemed more willing to hang around the habitat banks. Ecologists working on the project also reported that adders from the wider area were attracted to the release pens, possibly

A digger puts the finishing touches to the bank

Reed bundles are placed in position along the bank

following the airborne scent given off by female adders during the mating season.

Some of the adders in the pen were determined enough to escape from the pens, but the paint marks meant they could be identified and returned into the penned-off habitats.

An interesting observation was recorded when the two main release pens were linked by a corridor using further reptile fencing which was bridged over a small ditch to allow the two populations to mix. A yellow marked animal was found within the red marked animal's enclosure within a few days and the onset of a combat display was captured on video and camera (see photographs).

This was not the only incident of combat observed. Several other males were also observed in combat and mating behaviour, and mate-guarding was also witnessed.

From the initial results it seems that a small adder population had been removed successfully from danger and relocated to a prepared habitat where they settled and went through their natural behaviour until such time as the fences were removed and the adders were allowed to move back out into the farmland surrounding the new habitats. New-born adders were also found on the 'created' banks in the late summer or early autumn, suggesting that gravid females had stayed around the new habitats. It is hoped that further surveys will be undertaken to monitor the movements, abundance and distribution of relocated adders in relation to habitat creation and within the redeveloped areas.

The project will continue to work with the landowners managing the site for the next ten years, with follow-up surveys to determine the success of this strategy. I hope that the project will become an important example of how adders should be treated within mitigation projects throughout the UK.

Jon Cranfield *was a founder member of the Essex Amphibian & Reptile Group. He runs a wildlife consultancy called Herpetologic Ltd specialising in the conservation of reptiles and amphibians. He is the Vice Chair of the Amphibian & Reptile groups of the UK (ARG UK).*

Acknowledgements
Christian Whiting & Helen Booth and all who have worked on the Broadland Flood Alleviation Project (www.bfap.org), Ray Cranfield, Jamie Leek, John Baker, Bob Stebbings, Tony Phelps, Steve Langham, Lee Brady, Gareth Matthes and Kevin Morgan.

Are adder numbers declining?

Chris Monk

For some years there has been evidence of a decline in the adder population of the UK particularly in the Midlands and South East of England. Many sites that were reported to have adders in the 1970s and 1980s now appear to have none, whilst at others the situation is not clear.

The main reasons for the perceived decline are thought to be fragmentation of their habitat due to changes in agricultural and land management practices; development including the creation of barriers such as new roads; and continued persecution by a few people. This is despite the adder being protected under the *Wildlife and Countryside Act* from deliberate or intentional killing and injuring.

In order to check whether there is a significant national decline or just a collection of unrelated local problems, a project was devised in 2005 by the Herpetological Conservation Trust (now Amphibian and Reptile Conservation) and English Nature. Called *Make the Adder Count*, the project was based on asking experienced volunteers to go out and count their local adder population. The adder is most noticeable when it first emerges from hibernation in the spring, as on suitable days it will spend long periods lying out basking. Later in the spring, after mating time, adders are much more active and become dispersed across their habitat, making them more difficult to locate and count. Therefore the project asked the volunteers to record the highest number of adders seen at one time either at individual sites or by following a standard path through their habitat.

The aim was for the volunteers to visit sites at least three, but preferably more, times to record the highest number of snakes seen; the more visits there were, the greater the chance that the true maximum number of snakes would be recorded. The survey involved no handling or close approach to adders, which could disturb them, but only careful observation from a distance. By pooling all the results across the country and over several years, it would enable any national trends in adder populations to be identified.

Based on similar volunteer surveys for bird populations, it was known that at least 100 sites being surveyed each year for a decade would enable trends to be detected. In Kent there was already an established project being run by the Kent Reptile and

Amphibian Group investigating the decline of the adder, so the national project hoped to find volunteers to look at other parts of the country.

In Derbyshire and the Peak District there was known to be a population of adders in a certain part of the Peak District National Park. A small area of what was thought to be the main population of adders had already been surveyed and the snakes counted by the National Park rangers about a decade previously. The remainder of the area had not been studied for nearly a quarter of a century but occasional sightings by ramblers, rock climbers and naturalists on the moors suggested that they were still present in a more widespread area. With no existing experienced surveyors in the area, a volunteer from the county's Amphibian & Reptile Group decided to try and carry out the Project survey technique in 2005. Luckily one of the National Park's rangers who had taken part in their 1995 survey also agreed to help out, so the Project started out with two people.

At the end of that first year the survey had proved a success and the researchers' visits to neighbouring areas had already resulted in sightings of other clusters of adders. When the Herpetological Conservation Trust undertook a review of the success of the *Make the Adder Count* project at the end of the first year, the information from the Peak District National Park contributed more than 25% of the hibernation sites surveyed nationally.

But in order to continue the survey in the future and also to follow up all reports and sightings of adders in the wider Peak District, more than two people were obviously required. Therefore we needed to engage more volunteers and organise some basic training for them to show them how to look for adders and when to do it. Starting in 2006 and every spring since, the Derbyshire Amphibian and Reptile Group has organised a training day on the moors and encouraged people to commit to go out a few times and survey the sites that they were shown. This proved very successful, with over 20 people taking part and submitting counts to enable us to continue playing a major part in the national project. Some volunteers only managed to help for one year and even those who have not helped after the training day have learnt about this interesting snake. A few have become regular participants every year and avid adder enthusiasts, eagerly waiting for each spring to go out and be the first to see an adder that season and to search out new areas to find new hibernation sites.

As the surveys have developed and become more widely known, so details of casual adder sightings by members of the public have been passed on and followed up by the survey volunteers. Adders seen crossing, or found dead, on roads, watched swimming across streams and observed basking next to footpaths have all led to the discovery of population groups in nearby moorland.

There have been quite a few sightings on one particular road over several years, indicating that adders are crossing from the moorland where they are found in the early spring into the adjacent wet fen for the summer. As the fen is too wet for them to hibernate, they cross the road back to the drier ground in the autumn.

In its first six years, the adder population survey has revealed that almost all the 25 square kilometre block of moorland is suitable for adders and that some of the largest numbers are found outside the area previously thought by the National Park to be the main population stronghold. Indeed although most adders hibernate in small communal groups or in dispersed groups covering a distinct geographical area, individual adders may be found emerging from hibernation almost anywhere on the moorland. Approximately 40 main hibernation areas have been identified and some of the more remote areas of the moor have not yet been surveyed.

Bracken is perceived as a problem plant on many heathlands and moors but has been found to be a key location for adders in many parts of the Peak District moors. Where long-established bracken has built up to give banks of brown bracken mould up to one metre in height, with the previous year's dead stems and fronds sticking out of the top, the adders are using such banks as hibernation and basking sites.

Interestingly the adders are not just using the most sheltered locations as hibernation sites but are being found on the highest and most exposed tops of the gritstone edges. There despite being exposed to the wind from almost all directions, they have emerged from hibernation and can be found basking in small depressions which have their own micro-climates whilst the wind severely batters their human surveyor watching from a short distance away.

The Peak District Project has revealed some differences between the adders there and at other studied sites in England. In particular the Peak District adders do not appear to be as faithful to their hibernation sites as adders studied in Dorset and other lowland sites. Even over just a few years of the surveys, some of the Peak District hibernation sites have declined in adder numbers, some even becoming abandoned, whilst at other sites in the same area, numbers have increased. At a few sites there are significant annual variations in numbers, with up to a dozen snakes being seen one year and none the next. Their return a couple of years later suggests that they are using a different, as yet unfound, site for hibernation in the intervening years.

Overall the success of the project in the Peak District has been thanks to the dedication of those volunteering to spend their time surveying and counting this attractive snake. They have carried out the most intensive survey to date for the adder in this part of the country and have proved that at present it appears to be flourishing and occupying a significant, large block of moorland.

Whether this applies to adders generally across the UK will only become apparent as the *Make the Adder Count* project collects sufficient data over a long enough period of years to be able to detect national trends.

Chris Monk *is Secretary of the Derbyshire Amphibian and Reptile Group and the Derbyshire County Recorder. He has been studying adders in the Peak District National Park for many years.*

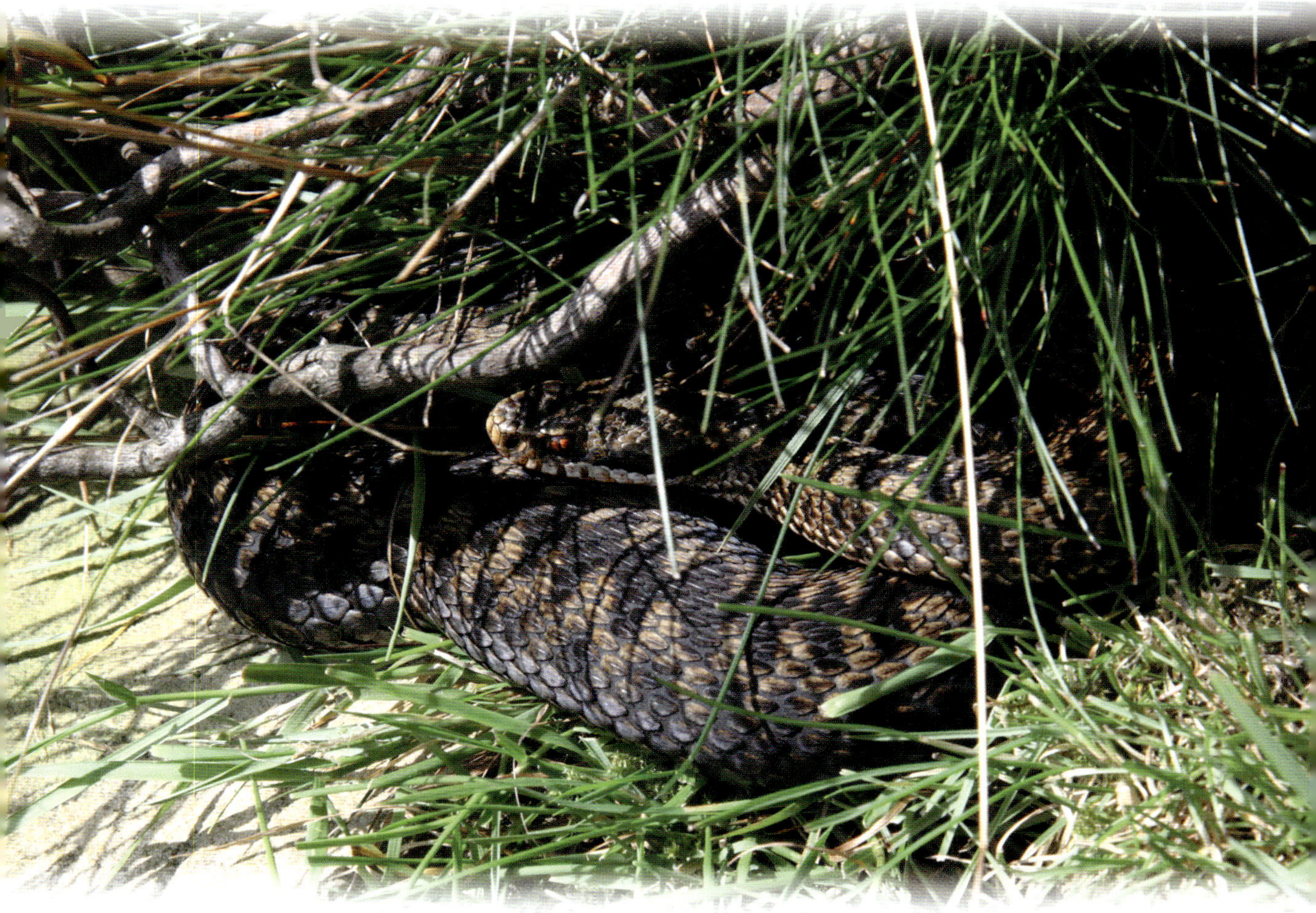

Acknowledgements

The publishers wish to thank the following people who have contributed photos to this book: David Mason for the hedgehog and badger (page 74), Jon Cranfield for the grass snake (page 11) and the habitat work photos (page 115) and John Baker for the smooth snake (page 13). We are also grateful to the five contributors, Sylvia Sheldon, Christopher Bradley, John Baker, Jon Cranfield and Chris Monk, whose essays in the latter part of the book throw interesting light on a number of specialist areas in adder work.

Useful Organisations

British Herpetological Society
11 Strathmore Place, Montrose
Angus DD10 8LQ
www.thebhs.org
info@thebhs.org

Amphibian & Reptile Conservation Trust (ARC Trust)
Main office: 655a Christchurch Road,
Boscombe, Bournemouth, Dorset BH1 4AP
(01202) 391319
enquiries@arc-trust.org

Make the Adder Count
(a national survey co-ordinated by ARC Trust – see above)
www.narrs.org.uk/addercount.htm
enquiries@arc-trust.org

Add an Adder
(a national survey co-ordinated by ARC Trust – see above)
www.adder.org.uk
(enter your sightings via the website)

Amphibian & Reptile Groups of the UK (ARG UK)
c/o ARC Trust, 655a Christchurch Road, Boscombe,
Bournemouth, Dorset BH1 4AP
www.arguk.org

National Amphibian and Reptile Recording Scheme (NARRS)
is coordinated by the ARC Trust (see details above)

Derbyshire Reptile and Amphibian Group
(adder surveys, etc)
www.derbyshirearg.co.uk
secretary@derbyshirearg.co.uk

Surrey Reptile and Amphibian Group (SARG)
www.surrey-arg.org.uk/SARG/SARG.asp

Kent Reptile and Amphibian Group (KRAG)
Adders in Decline Project
www.kentarg.org/projects/adders-in-decline-project
(submit your sightings online)

Herefordshire Reptile and Amphibian Team (HART)
What's That Snake? project
Project Co-ordinator: Nigel Hand
c/o The Hereford Nature Trust 01432 356872
www.herefordhart.org

Herpetologic Ltd
(an independent consultancy specialising in reptile conservation)
38 Nursery Road, Alresford, Winchester
Hampshire SO24 9JR
www.herpetologic.co.uk

Also published by Merlin Unwin Books
www.merlinunwin.co.uk

The Hare
Jill Mason £20

The Otter
James Williams £20

The Naturalist's Bedside Book
BB £17.99

The Countryman's Bedside Book
BB £18.99

The Best of BB
BB £18.99

Mushrooming Without Fear
Alexander Schwab £14.99